D1454282

WATFORD

HERTFORDSHIRE ARCHIVES & LOCAL STUDIES

The
History
Press

First published 2012

The History Press
The Mill, Brimscombe Port
Stroud, Gloucestershire, GL5 2QG
www.thehistorypress.co.uk

ISBN 978 0 7524 6556 2

Typesetting and origination by The History Press
Printed in Great Britain

CONTENTS

New Street, a quiet corner near St Mary's churchyard, Watford, *c.* 1880. It has now been replaced by the hustle and bustle of a multi-storey car park. [WatSerC 0098-00-01]

INTRODUCTION

The landscape around modern Watford has an ancient history. A major archaeological project at The Grove undertaken in 2000–1 revealed evidence for continuous human occupation from the Bronze Age over 4,000 years ago. Roman villa sites have been identified near Munden and Hamper Mill. The valley of the River Gade has very fertile, easily farmed soils which would have attracted these early settlers.

Some of the earliest written evidence refers to Cassio or Cashio, a large estate covering Cassiobury Park, The Grove and what is now the town of Watford with extensive woodland to the west. This estate was granted to St Albans Abbey in the mid-tenth century (c. 950) and was the largest and the most profitable of the abbey's holdings. In Domesday Book (1086) Cashio is described as being 20 hides (approximately 2,400 acres) in extent with sufficient woodland to accommodate 1,000 pigs. There were also four mills, 22 ploughs and 52 people are listed, including two slaves. Recent archaeological evidence has suggested that the manor house of Cashio was located near The Grove, north of the area now known as Cassiobury Park where the later mansion once stood.

After the Dissolution of St Albans Abbey in 1539 this estate came to the crown and was granted by Henry VIII in 1545 to Richard Morrison. It was inherited by the Capel family (later Earls of Essex) in the seventeenth century and this family continued to own the estate until the early twentieth century. Succeeding generations developed the park and mansion and several famous landscape gardeners and architects worked at Cassiobury. At the beginning of the nineteenth century the 5th Earl of Essex employed James Wyatt to remodel his house in the Gothic style and Humphry Repton to redesign his park. As wealthy landlords the Earls of Essex took a leading part in Watford's local affairs and his house would have been full of books, pictures and wonderful carvings. At the 1841 census the earl employed a total of 27 people including a cook and governess at the house, four men resident at the stables and a gardener and his family at the garden cottage. A description of the house and estate published in 1837 describes the park and woodland with its deer, sheep and peacocks, and the gardens including lawns, a Chinese garden, hothouses, an orangery, ponds and fountains. The house had 84 rooms, including four libraries.

The town of Watford with its church was probably founded in the early twelfth century on the higher ground to the east of Cassiobury along the road from London. The county historian Henry Chauncy, writing in 1700, states that a weekly market was granted to the town by Henry I (between 1100 and 1135). This would provide the economic foundation for the future development of Watford as a trading centre for local goods and agricultural produce destined for London. The Lay Subsidy tax list of 1307 lists 109 tax payers in Watford from which we can estimate that the local population had risen to nearly 500. In 1331 the abbot undertook a survey of all his manors to record what rents and services were owed to him and what customs there were. From this document, now held at Hertfordshire Archives and Local Studies (HALS), we learn that, as well as a school, Watford had a 'cornereshopp' next to the churchyard for which the tenant Henry Cokedell paid 8d per year in rent. This would have occupied a prominent and desirable position in the market place and therefore was probably a very profitable concern.

Daniel Defoe, writing in 1778, describes Watford as a 'genteel market town, . . . very long, having but one street.' Watford's main high street is indeed almost 1½ miles long. In the sixteenth century to travel north from London, 15 miles away, the River Colne first had to be forded to the south of the town. The main road from St Albans to Rickmansworth also crosses the High Street at the north end. Increased trade was brought to the town by the opening of the Grand Junction Canal through Cassiobury and The Grove in 1796. But even at the beginning of the nineteenth century Watford was still a relatively small market town, rural in character, a mail coach leaving for London every morning. In 1821 the town population was 2,960, many people living in the overcrowded alleys and courtyards off the High Street. The London & Birmingham Railway Company opened their station at Watford in 1837 and from this time the town slowly began to expand. In 1841 the population was 3,697 but over 30 per cent were still working in agriculture and related trades. The remainder were employed in the three silk mills, straw plait and paper making or malting and brewing.

A Local Board of Health was formed in 1850 to provide a safe water supply and attempt to alleviate the insanitary nature of the overcrowded town highlighted in a damning report to the Government of 1849. The first new streets to be developed were King Street to the west of the High Street and Queens Road to the east. The opening of the railway branch lines to St Albans and Rickmansworth later in the century prompted landowners to offer up further areas for building. Estates at Harwoods Farm and Callowland were developed after 1891. An Urban District Council was formed in 1894 and the area of the town was extended to include a portion of Bushey and the hamlet of Oxhey. By 1901 Watford was the largest town in Hertfordshire with a total population of 32,559. Watford proudly became a Borough Council in 1922 and the services it now provides include the provision of parks, housing and leisure facilities. Local Government reorganisation in 1974 saw the creation of an enlarged Watford Borough.

By the mid-twentieth century Watford was far more of an industrial town with huge factories involved in printing and engineering. Pioneering printing processes were developed in Watford and Odhams and the Sun Engraving Company became household names. By 1970 Odhams employed 3,000 people. Scammell in west Watford and Rolls-Royce at Leavesden were particularly important for engineering. Many buildings have been demolished to make way for new roads and car parks to cope with the massive increase in traffic. Some changes reflect a national trend such as the pedestrianisation of Watford's High Street and provision of cycle routes in the late 1990s. Excellent communication links and a large resident workforce encouraged companies to locate their premises in Watford. Their recent demise has changed the character of the town and huge areas have been redeveloped yet again for housing. Watford is no longer renowned for its beer, printing or engineering. To many people it is best known for its football team and the Harlequin shopping centre.

The references for all of the images reproduced here have been included in the captions. Those which simply say 'HALS' are to be found in our library collections. HALS holds a wealth of documents and photographs relating to Watford from earliest times to the present day.
For more information visit our website: **www.hertsdirect.org/hals**

1

SHOPPING

Of these buildings photographed in June 1898 at 210 Lower High Street, only what was Capell's
Furniture Warehouse is still standing, now without the left-hand bay windows. On the right is one of the
200 branches of the International Tea Company found on many Victorian High Streets.
Next is W. Wright the coachbuilder, then Fox Alley and The Fox pub, owned by Benskin, whose brewery
stands just a short distance along the street to the right. Taylors is a somewhat scruffy drapers shop.
Further to the left are more hostelries – The Swan (adjoining Capell's), The Holly Bush and, in the
distance, The Rising Sun. [Acc 3556]

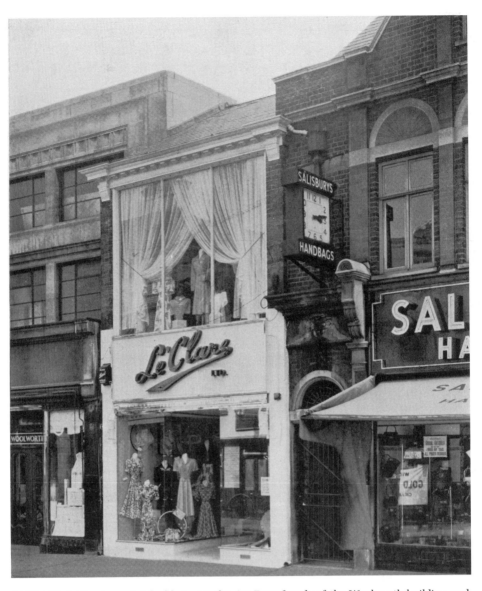

At 116 High Street, sandwiched between the Art Deco façade of the Woolworth building and Salisbury's Handbags, is the unusual shop front of Mr Goldstein's ladies' outfitters 'Le Clare', displaying the latest in 1950s fashion. In this 1951 photograph, the shop's upper floor has large modern-looking windows. Earlier photographs show that these windows, with some minor alterations, had been in place since at least 1893. [DE/X269/B54]

Opposite, bottom: 'There are few shopping centres in the country which are more popular than Watford' promised the auction catalogue when the Watford branch of Dolcis shoe shop was advertised for sale in April 1952. It further boasted that 'The property occupies the very finest retail trading position in this well-known and popular Hertfordshire town.' The shop stood at 114 a and b High Street, next to the entrance to St Mary's churchyard in the very heart of the town centre. The shops to the left are Style & Mantle gowns and J. Lyons & Co. caterers. There is still a branch of Dolcis in the modern Harlequin Centre. [DE/X269/B55]

This busy junction of Queens Road and King Street with the High Street suffered from particularly heavy traffic jams. When the ring road was constructed in the early 1960s in an attempt to deal with this problem, traffic approaching from the Lower High Street was diverted left into King Street. Woolworths had existed here since 1916 but as the store expanded, the Art Deco building was replaced with this edifice in 1966. It finally closed in 1990 and was later demolished. The shell of the Barclays Bank building on the left still stands. [HALS]

Looking south at the
Tuesday livestock market
in the Market Place,
c. 1880. The auctioneer
can just be seen under a
makeshift canopy outside
The Compasses. The
building on the right, in
between The Compasses
and the white bulk of
The Rose & Crown Hotel,
was demolished to make
way for the construction
of Market Street in 1889.
Second on the left is the
Bucks and Oxon Bank,
which was shortly to be
rebuilt. [Acc 3556]

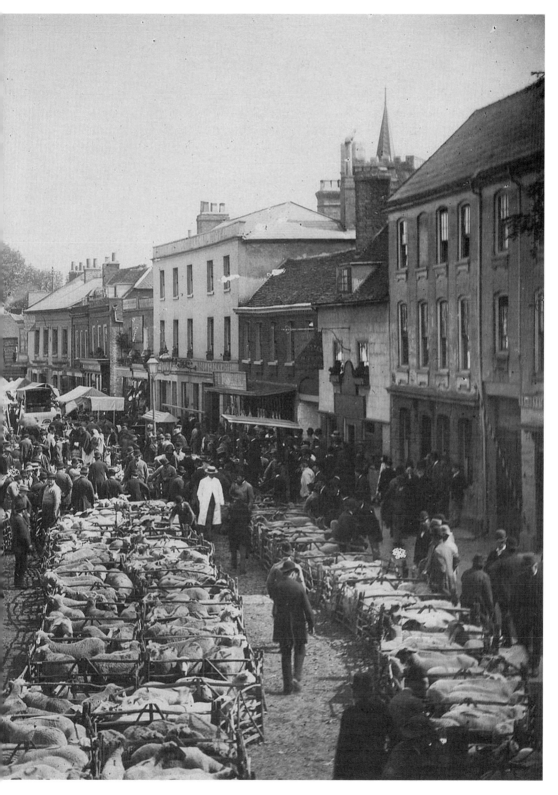

The same view of the Market Place in 1927 with the Saturday merchandise market in full swing. The entrance to Market Street is to the right of the remodelled Rose & Crown Hotel. The Bucks and Oxon Bank is now a Lloyds Bank and has a new, grander façade. Next door is Roger and Gowlett, heating and electrical engineers and ironmongers, who remained here until at least 1938. Only the bank just mentioned and one building on the right-hand side now remain from this 1927 view. In 1928 the livestock market moved to Market Street, and the stalls to land behind The Essex Arms on the left, later becoming a fully covered market. [CV/WATF179]

Looking north from the corner of High Street and Clarendon Road in the 1920s, showing an advert for Trewin Brothers. Over the road Arthur East, a corn and coal merchant, also supplied animal fodder, poultry meals and dog biscuits. Next door, E. B. Burridge the tailor limited his trade to 'a certain class with no ready made goods being kept'. Only the building that is now Jackson Jewellers, 22–6 High Street (in the centre with a child in the doorway) survives today. [WatSerC 0325-00-02]

Opposite, bottom: A view down Market Street from the High Street in about 1900. At numbers 4 and 6, Reeve & Co.'s two shops – an outfitters and a furniture store – make full use of the pavement space. Advertising hoardings can be seen above the shop fronts – one showing a gentleman in suit and bowler hat. On the right is Birds Coffee Tavern and Dining Rooms which is situated on the corner of the Wellstones, and to the left is A. E. Weller, wine and beer merchant. Just visible above the rooftops is the spire of Holy Rood Church. [HALS]

The late 1950s and busy Clarendon Road corner is now controlled by traffic lights. Garners bakery was in business here from 1938 until 1978. To the left are MacFisheries, Willerby the tailors and Dewhurst the butchers. These single-storey shops were knocked down for redevelopment in the mid-1980s. The large building to the left of Dewhurst used to house Watford's famous department store Clement's, which had been in business since 1898. Note the police call box standing next to the traffic light. [HrtCpl-0169-01-02]

Although Beechen Grove is now part of the ring road, the old course of the road ran along Gartlet Road (as it is known today), down the lower end of Estcourt Road, past the bottom of Sutton Road and into Derby Road. This peaceful view shows the little cluster of cottages that used to stand to the rear of the Beechen Grove Baptist Church. The junction with Sutton Road is on the right. Still a landmark today, the Baptist church, seen here rising above the rooftops, was opened in 1878. [Wat SerC 0166-00-01]

Opposite, bottom: The Cawdell family had traded in the town since about 1880. In 1905 James Cawdell's drapery and furnishing shop opened at 71 High Street next to The Essex Arms Hotel. Both buildings were demolished in the early 1930s. The rebuilt Cawdells, shown here, had a mighty Art Deco façade, quite distinct from the surrounding shops, although Woolworths, further down the High Street, was a smaller example of the style. The clock was a later addition. Cawdells was demolished in the 1970s to make way for the entrance to Charter Place. The smaller classical style Midland Bank building still stands today. [HrtCpl-0159-01-02]

Looking north along the Hempstead Road, this deceptively rural scene is Cassio Hamlet in the early twentieth century. Only a stone's throw from the expanding High Street and new housing, Cassio Hamlet would eventually be completely overtaken by the developer. This string of cottages was to make way for the Town Hall, public baths and Technical College. The Horns public house can just be seen before the bend in the road and still stands, now opposite Watford Central Library opened in 1928. Further along from the Horns was another pub, The Dog, which managed to avoid demolition until 1970. [WatSerC 0044-00_01]

Cassio Hamlet, Hempstead Road looking south towards the High Street, St Albans Road and Rickmansworth Road crossroads before the construction of a roundabout in 1936. The Town Hall was to be built to the right of the picture in 1938. Behind the fence on the left was Little Nascot House, a mother and baby clinic in the 1920s, demolished for road widening in 1959. The Parade is only partially developed. In the distance is the domed Plaza cinema which opened in 1929. The impressive National Westminster Bank, glimpsed between the trees, dates from 1931. [WatSerC 0321-00_02]

High Street traffic in 1939 – bicycles were simply left by the kerb and the absence of yellow lines meant motorists could park outside the shop of their choice. Zebra crossings were yet to be introduced to British roads so pedestrians had to fend for themselves. Shops on the left include Findlater's wine and spirits, J. & F. Stone lighting and radio, Christmas' motor engineers, Buck's restaurant and confectioners and Wren's leather goods. [WatGrv 0079-00_06]

Cornishman Arthur Trewin, seen here on the right in about 1910, came to Watford in 1880 and purchased a small draper's shop in Queens Road. He was also a Sunday School teacher at Watford Wesleyan Methodist Church. A new Wesleyan church in Villiers Road, Bushey, opened in 1886 and in 1890 Mr Trewin became their afternoon school superintendent, a post he held for 22 years. In addition he acted as secretary for the new church built in London Road, Bushey, in 1904–5. On the left are the Revd A. J. Beamwich, pastor from 1908 to 1911 and Miss Rankin, deaconess. [NM7Q/59/17]

In 1887 Trewins moved to these newly built premises called Osborne House at 26–8 Queens Road, seen here decorated for the coronation of King Edward VII in 1902. Their stock included household linens, furs, children's hosiery and trimmings. Shortly afterwards Arthur's younger brother Henry joined the business and it became known as Trewin Brothers. In 1918 the business was sold to Gordon Selfridge who ran it until selling to John Lewis in January 1940. [John Lewis Partnership Archive Collection]

The furniture department, early 1930s. By the 1960s the store had doubled in size and employed 300 staff. The Partnership had also acquired Kinghams, a long-established Watford chain of grocery shops, later to become part of Waitrose. In 1990 Trewins moved to the newly built Harlequin Shopping Centre and in September 2001 was renamed John Lewis Watford. [John Lewis Partnership Archive Collection]

Opposite: It's the early 1930s and the millinery and gowns and haberdashery departments are decorated for Christmas. [John Lewis Partnership Archive Collection]

On 2 January 1941 a bomb caused extensive damage to Trewin brothers' toy department – luckily after Christmas! [WatGrv 0193-00_15]

Further along the road from Trewins also stood the extensive premises of Francis J. Harding, Broadway House, 47 Queens Road, ladies' and children's outfitters, fancy drapers and milliners. Mr Harding purchased the property in 1922 and his trade figures doubled after dressing his windows for the first time, and almost doubled again when a new front was installed. An advertising feature of 1931 proclaims the business 'is a model of what a retail establishment of this type should be . . . Mr Harding has always sought to supply the right goods at the right time and at the right price. Nothing of inferior quality finds its place among the extensive stocks'! [Acc 4945]

Right: The Arcade. [Acc 4945]

Below: Francis J. Harding knitwear and ladies underclothing, glove and hosiery departments. [Acc 4945]

Thomas Horton's butcher's shop at 115 St Albans Road, *c.* 1890. The family had traded in St Albans Road since at least 1872 and from 1886 also had a shop at no. 94. For a time they had another at 116 Whippendell Road employing a total of seven assistant butchers. Thomas died in 1899 but family members continued to run the business until about 1964. [Acc 5067 Rose Freeman]

Thomas Horton, his wife Jane and their family, *c.* 1890. [Acc 5067 Rose Freeman]

Montagu Bateman's chemist shop stood at 76 St Albans Road, near the junction with Station Road and Langley Road. An advert for the shop in the 1905 edition of *Peacock's Directory* for Watford tells us he sold 'purest drugs, chemical, toilet and nursery articles'. Prescriptions 'both English and foreign' were dispensed, which may account for his claim to be chemist to the late Khédive Ismail (Viceroy of Egypt). In addition, photography was fast becoming a popular hobby, so Mr Bateman found a business opportunity in catering to the amateur photographer by developing negatives and selling photographic equipment. [CV/WATF211]

The idea behind a Co-operative Society began in 1844 in Rochdale as a business owned by its customers which reinvested profits in the local community. There are now over 5,000 such stores across the UK and customers are still given a share in the profits affectionately known as 'divi'. The Watford Society moved from premises in Leavesden Road to St Albans Road in 1898. This Art Deco building was erected in 1929 and still exists today but is no-longer a Co-op. When this photograph was taken in 1931 the store employed over 520 people and proudly claimed to return over £50,000 in dividend to its members. Later it moved to Gade House at 14 High Street but by 1996 this too had closed. [HALS]

2

HEALTH & EDUCATION

These almshouses in Church Street were erected in 1580 by Francis, 2nd Earl of Bedford, to house eight poor widows from Watford and Chenies in Buckinghamshire. They are now Grade II listed and are the oldest inhabited dwellings remaining in Watford. [Acc 3556]

The London Orphan Asylum was founded in 1813 by the philanthropist Dr Andrew Reed 'to maintain, clothe and educate respectable children of either sex . . . whose fathers had lost their lives in the Army, Navy and Marine Services'. The Prince of Wales visited Watford on 15 July 1869 to lay the foundation stone and the children moved from London in 1871. This photograph shows the girls' wing and playground in about 1900. In 1939, the school was renamed Reed's School and in 1940 was requisitioned for use as an army hospital. The children were evacuated and never returned to Watford, finally settling at Cobham, Surrey, in 1946. The buildings are now Reeds Housing Estate. [WatDwn 0016-00_01]

Built at a cost of £17,000, the Victoria Cottage Hospital in Vicarage Road was opened by Lady Clarendon in 1886. It accommodated nine beds but in 1897, to mark the Diamond Jubilee of Queen Victoria, a six-bed ward and operating theatre were added. In memory of the Coronation of King Edward VII in 1902, the hospital was enlarged further, with two more six-bed wards, dining rooms and staff accommodation. [WatSerB 0050-00_01]

Opened by the Adventists in May 1912, the Stanborough Park Sanatorium, Garston, was 'modelled throughout on the latest ideas of sanitation and hygiene'. Practising hydrotherapy (formerly hydropathy), the use of water for pain relief and treating illness, the sanatorium facilities also included physiotherapy, radiotherapy, a small operating theatre and a maternity wing. The creation of the National Health Service in 1948 led to an initial decline in private healthcare and after suffering years of financial losses, the sanatorium finally closed its doors in 1968. [HALS]

The Watford and District Peace Memorial Hospital, Rickmansworth Road, was opened in June 1925. Here it is decorated for the coronation in 1953. The clock over the porch was donated by Alexander Hicks, licensee of The Rose & Crown Hotel, Market Place, and was installed between May and November 1931. The hospital was closed in 1986 and amalgamated with the Watford General Hospital, Vicarage Road. The original Memorial building still stands and it reopened in 1996 as the Peace Hospice. [WatLns 0400-00_04]

By 1937 the 87 beds provided at the hospital had proved totally inadequate for the needs of the rapidly expanding town. The Duke and Duchess of Kent opened a new ward and nurses' home to be known as Knutsford House on 27 October 1937. [Acc 4237]

The Free School, adjoining St Mary's churchyard, was endowed by Mrs Elizabeth Fuller in 1704 to educate 40 poor boys and 20 girls from the parish of Watford. The architecture is a prime example of the Queen Anne style and is Grade II listed. The school itself closed in 1882, but from its legacy developed Watford Boys' and Watford Girls' Grammar Schools. The building, now renamed Church House, continues to be used for parochial purposes. [WatDwn 0031-00_01]

This photograph of the interior of the Free School is dated September 1925 and was taken by local architect and photographer Andrew Whitford Anderson. He had moved to Watford from London in 1892 and opened an office at 16 Westland Road in 1900, subsequently moving to the High Street, first at 28 and later at 58. He died on 27 November 1950 but not before amassing a huge collection of photographs which are now housed at Hertfordshire Archives. [Acc 3556]

This school founded by George, 5th Earl of Essex (died 1839), for sixty boys and girls of the working classes, and open to all denominations, was wholly maintained at the earl's expense. It was situated on the Cassiobury Estate near the great entrance gates of the park. This wonderful image shows what appears to be wash day and lots of cheeky smiles. [MSC 0050-00_03]

Built in 1881 in Chalk Hill Oxhey to accommodate 260 children, this school was doubled in size in 1899. The average attendance in 1902 was 216 girls and 175 infants increasing to 246 girls and 200 infants by 1906. This photograph shows the staff in 1902. Back row, left to right: Miss Hogetts, Miss Hirst, -?-, -?-. Middle row: Miss Schultz, Miss Featherby, Mrs Adelaide L. Pine (Infant Mistress), Miss Summerfield, Miss Allitt, Miss Pitkin. Front row: Miss Pine, Miss Good, -?-. [Acc 3556]

Watford Public Library and School of Science and Art opened in 1874 in Queens Road. A prospectus of 1923 shows that the school offered a wide range of classes in fine art, commercial art (including poster design), crafts such as art, needlework, embroidery and lace, trades including process engraving, house painting and decoration, typography, millinery and dress decoration and commercial subjects such as book-keeping, shorthand and typewriting in both day and evening classes. The President was the Earl of Clarendon.
[WatLns 0337-00_04]

Drawing class in the School of Art, 1923. [DE/X760/1]

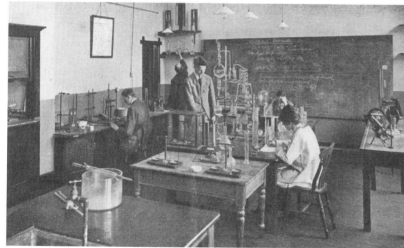

The physical laboratory, 1923. [DE/X760/1]

A shorthand class, 1923. [DE/X760/1]

The library had moved out of the Queens Road building in 1928 but even this did not provide enough accommodation to meet demand for classes. Plans for a new Technical College were proposed in 1935, to be built near the Town Hall on Hempstead Road. Building began in 1938, but ceased in 1939. Although only partially completed it was used as a Government Training Centre during the Second World War. In 1948 the technology department moved in, and was joined by a newly formed printing department in 1950. Finally completed in 1952, it was officially opened by Lieutenant-General Sir Ronald M. Weeks on 15 May 1953. Now known as West Herts College, this imposing building stands empty awaiting its fate after a new building was erected nearby in 2010. [DE/X760/3]

Commerce department typewriting room, 1953, 'fitted with acoustic tiles to reduce noise, and equipped with specially designed desks, duplicating machines, an electric recording machine and a filing cabinet fitted with suspended files'. [DE/X760/3]

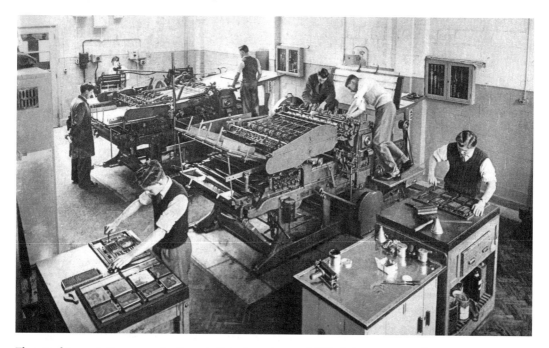

The machine printing room in the printing department, 1953. Printing was still a major industry in Watford at this time and the college catered for all sections of the industry. Separate rooms were provided for bookbinding, letterpress, photo-process and a typography design studio. [DE/X760/3]

The cookery and housecraft room, 1953. A model restaurant was also provided so that catering students could receive training in counter service and waiting. Needlecraft subjects such as needlework, dressmaking and tailoring were also taught. [DE/X760/3]

The carpentry and joinery shop in the building department, 1953. In addition there were two workshops for brickwork and plumbing, two drawing offices and a building science laboratory. [DE/X760/3]

3

AT WORK

Throughout the First World War there were two munitions factories in Watford run by the Ministry of Munitions of War – the No. 25 National Filling factory in Bushey Mill Lane and the National Filling Factory, Watford No. 1 (Trench Warfare) on Imperial Way/Balmoral Road. [Acc 4573]

Bombs, grenades, smoke canisters and small arms ammunition were manufactured in Watford. Just as in similar factories in the Second World War much of the work was undertaken by women. Men were employed to make the wooden packing cases and see to their despatch. They were dangerous places and accidents and fires claimed the lives of five Watford people between 1914 and 1918. [Acc 4573]

Opposite: The firm of North & Sons began as watchmakers in Soho, London, before moving to Watford in 1903. They manufactured speedometers and magnetos in their factory on Whippendell Road, employing over 500 people. Workers were mainly men, although six women were engaged in engraving speedometer dials. Their magnetos were used on Rolls-Royce engines and their speedometers on Malcolm Campbell's Bluebird when he achieved the world record speed of 245mph on Daytona Beach in 1931. The 1930s were a difficult time for the industry and the company was forced to close in 1933. The factory was bought by Sun Engraving, who renamed it Rembrandt House. [Acc 3547]

The Sun Engraving Company Limited (Sun Printers Ltd from 1945) moved from London to Whippendell Road in 1919, expanding into the North & Sons factory in 1933. They pioneered the development of four colour printing techniques and by 1935 were producing 70 per cent of Britain's mass-market magazines, including *Woman's Own, Picture Post, Country Life, Farmers Weekly*, and in 1962 the very successful first ever weekly colour newspaper supplement – the *Sunday Times* colour magazine. The company boomed from 1,000 employees in 1919 to more than 3,600 in 1963. Purchased by Robert Maxwell in 1981 it finally closed in 2004 and the buildings were demolished. [HALS]

Founded in London in 1894 as a newspaper group, Odhams was the biggest print works in England when it moved to North Watford in the 1930s. The Duke of Kent visited the new factory in April 1937 and watched the production of the official coronation programme. The striking Press Hall was built in 1954 and the innovative clock tower housed a water tank for use in the printing process. It closed in 1983 but was used by Robert Maxwell as a printing plant for the *Daily Mirror* for a short time. The end of an era for Watford, a supermarket has now been built on part of the site. [Acc 4237]

The premises of James Darvill, builder and undertaker, 12 Nascot Street, in about 1900. Trade directory advertisements declare that the firm was established in 1888 and from 1929 became James Darvill & Son. From about 1947 the firm was run by Harold G. Darvill. The last owner was Alan Darvill who at his retirement in 2011 closed the business, which was still trading from the same premises in Nascot Street. [Acc 3556]

Clement Childs' hairdresser's shop in St Albans Road, *c.* 1905. As well as cutting hair, the sign in the window declares they sharpen razors, scissors and knives, re-cane chairs and re-cover umbrellas. One of Clement's sons, possibly the boy in the photograph, assisted his father in the shop and by the 1930s, the business was known as 'Childs and Childs'. Clement Childs senior died in 1958 at the ripe old age of ninety. [WatLns 0547-00-06]

A group of Watford police constables and their sergeant, early 1920s. Watford's first purpose-built police station was opened at King Street in 1889 and remained in use until 1940. The building had eight cells, an exercise yard, offices and residential accommodation. In 1922, three inspectors, a superintendent, ten sergeants and sixty-seven constables were based there. It later became the Sir Robert Peel pub which in turn closed in 2007. The building was recently saved from demolition. [Acc 3556]

The smiling staff of Watford Central Library in 1933. The new building in Hempstead Road took a year to construct and opened in December 1928. It was designed by H. A. Gold and W. Newman and cost over £20,000. Until then, the library shared a building in Queens Road with the School of Science and Art. The Borough Librarian, Mr G. R. Bolton, is pictured centre front. [WatSerC 0327-00_02]

A carefully posed picture in the watch room of Watford fire station in September 1939. During the Second World War the telephone and fire alarm systems were manned by women, while others were trained to drive the borough's ambulances based at the first-aid HQ behind the public baths in Hempstead Road. [WatGrv 0542-00-42]

Senior staff on the steps of the Town Hall making ready to read the proclamation for Queen Elizabeth II's coronation in 1953. From left to right are the Assistant Town Crier, Mr Bernard P. Lees; the Town Crier, Mr D. H. Bennett; the Mayor, Alderman A. G. Dillingham and the Town Clerk, Mr G. H. Hall. [Acc 3556]

An itinerant knife grinder, once a familiar sight in Watford's streets, would call house by house and for a fee sharpen knives, scissors or shears on his grinding wheel. He is standing outside the home of Miss Halsey, dressmaker. Trade directories for 1886 and 1890 list Mrs Annie Halsey and Miss Eliza Halsey, dressmakers at 4 King Street, Watford. By the census of 1891 Anna Halsey, a dressmaker and a widow, is still listed at 4 King Street together with her eight-year-old daughter Kate. [WatLns 0565-00_06]

The County Window Cleaning and Steam Carpet Beating Company acquired their New Road premises in 1938. This employee stands proudly beside his van having won a prize at the Watford carnival of May 1940. His offside headlamp is fitted with a wartime lamp deflector and unusually a low fitted fog lamp while the offside side light has been blacked out. EUR773 was first registered to the company on 7 June 1939 in the Motor Taxation Department at County Hall, Hertford. It is a Bedford PC 10/12cwt with a 4-cylinder engine of 1,442cc. [WatGrv 0430-00_34]

4

AT PLAY

This charming postcard is dated 5 July 1912. St Andrew's Church clock shows the time as
11 o'clock on what appears to be a leisurely, sunny day. The ladies in their skirts, blouses and large
flowery hats typify the pre-First World War era. Cycling became hugely popular in the 1890s with the
introduction of the safety bicycle and for women in particular, it was enormously liberating.
The corner seen here where Park Road and Church Road meet is largely unchanged today, although
houses have replaced the brick wall and hedge. [HALS]

These smart-looking chaps belong to the Watford Cycling Club and are posing outside the pavilion at the West Herts Ground, *c.* 1900. It became a sports ground in 1891 when Watford Football Club was granted a lease by the Earl of Essex for a nominal fee. The earl remained as its president for some years. At the time, there was a universal obsession for cycling clubs that lasted until the rise of the motor car. Note the penny farthing leaning against the fence. [WatLns 0181-00_03]

International Ladies Day at Oxhey Golf Club, October 1931. Pictured left to right are: Miss Joyce Wethered (Lady Heathcoat-Amory), one of the best known and highly successful lady golfers of her day who led the English team, Mrs Garon, Madame Munier and Madame Vagliano. This was the first match between ladies teams representing England and France and a crowd of nearly 5,000 people watched. The golf club existed from 1912 until 1946 and the club house is now the Brookdene Arms. [Acc 3970]

Members of the Watford Bowls Club at their opening season in May 1915. With many members serving at the front, the vast majority posing here are over enlisting age although many would have been engaged in duties such as special constables, or as members of the Volunteer Training Corps. [HALS]

The pond in the High Street, seen here in 1926, was obviously a favourite place to play. [WatSerC 0161-01_01]

When the Palace Theatre in Clarendon Road opened in 1908 its outside appearance was rather austere. Structural work in 1911 included the creation of the façade which remains in place and largely unaltered to this day – here one of the distinctive twin cupolas is being hoisted to the roof. To the right is L. Doyle, scale and weighing machine manufacturer, and to the left is a roller skating rink. Clarendon Road, built as a link between the Junction station and the High Street in 1864, was originally lined with large houses. [WatSerC 0023-00_01]

The Palace is now the oldest surviving Edwardian theatre in the region and is nationally recognised as a leading repertory theatre. Many famous actors have trod the Palace's boards, from Marie Lloyd to Helen Mirren. Here in January 1953 *Mother Goose* was coming to the end of a successful run. In 1992 the theatre named its new Corporate Hospitality Suite 'The John Mills Room' in honour of its president. It was closed between 2002 and 2004 for major refurbishment. [HrtCpl 0162-00_02]

Above: Even during the First World War leisure activities still took place. A very successful dance on Tuesday 19 January 1915 at the Kingham Hall, near Clarendon Road, was hosted by the Sergeants of the 6th and 7th (City of London) Battalions of the London Regiment. Dancing commenced at 7.30 p.m. and finished at half past midnight. The room was not overcrowded as only a limited number of invitations were issued, although nearly all the officers were present. [*Watford Illustrated* 23/1/1915]

Built by voluntary labour, the Trade Union Hall in Woodford Road was the scene of many meetings, dances, bazaars and entertainments. Members gave an enthusiastic welcome to Prime Minister Ramsay MacDonald when it was officially opened by him in 1931. [HALS]

The Nascot Arms' darts team pose proudly outside their pub in Stamford Road in July 1938. They had just won the Benskin's pub league scoring 44 points out of a possible 52. The pub had been built in 1866 by the brewer John Dyson, whose business was taken over by Benskin in 1867. [Acc 3883]

Boxing stars at the opening night of a skittle alley at the Queens Arms in St Albans Road, 1951. In aid of the Professional Boxers' Association, here we see, left to right: Laurie Buxton, Ralph Moss, Charles Sturt (the licensee), and Len Harvey. A large crowd raised £50 for the cause, which was attended by other well-known sportsmen and the former boxing referee and BBC commentator, Barrington Dalby. [Acc 3883]

During Watford's Warship Week of 1942, Cawdells department store pulled in the crowds with a circus in the basement of their premises in the High Street. Over 6,000 people paid the 3*d* entrance fee and proceeds went to the Peace Hospital. As well as a baby elephant, the audience were treated to the spectacle of two dogs riding a pony. [WatGrv 0528-00_41 and 0530-00_41]

Collecting pennies from the crowd at the August bank holiday carnival in 1942. The proceeds went to the Peace Memorial Hospital committee and the event, held at Cassiobury Park, attracted thousands of visitors who made the most of their 'Stay at Home Holidays'. Pictured to the right of the stretcher for collecting the cash is the Carnival Queen, Miss Betty Oliver. [WatGrv 0076-00_06]

The Greensward Traditional Dance Group celebrates the coronation of Queen Elizabeth II in June 1953 at the St Albans Road/Harebreaks corner, which is now a very busy junction. The Assistant Town Crier, Mr B. P. Lees, is watching from the left. [Acc 3556]

Opposite: Watford Public Library opened in 1874 as part of the School of Science and Art in Queens Road. It moved out in 1928 to its present home in Hempstead Road near the Town Hall and was officially opened by Sir Frederick G. Kenyon, Director and Principal Librarian of the British Museum. Originally only the lecture hall was upstairs, but the building was extended in the 1950s to complete the façade. [WatLns 0479-00_05 and 0537-00_06]

Watford's public baths on Hempstead Road were opened on 10 May 1933 and were believed to be the first to be electrically heated. The facility reopened in 2008 after major refurbishment. [WatLns 0097-00_02 and 0397-00_04]

An itinerant entertainer visited Watford in 1915. John Drayton of Leeds made the whole instrument himself, and travelled about the country with his wife and child to play it for his living. He is reported as saying that 'the open air life suits him better'. [*Watford Illustrated* 30 January 1915]

The Hertfordshire Canine Society Sanction show was held at the Clarendon Hall during the 1920s. Here Mrs Palmer is pictured with her alsatian Hammal, which took first prize. The Clarendon Hall, formerly the Agricultural Hall, stood near Clarendon Road and hosted magic lantern lectures and other shows. It declined after the Palace Theatre opened in 1908 and eventually became the Territorial Drill Hall and was demolished in the 1960s to make way for the ring road. [HALS]

5

AT WAR

Mounted Territorial units like the Hertfordshire Yeomanry needed huge numbers of horses on mobilisation in August 1914. Government horse-buyers scoured the countryside for them with powers to requisition. Here, in the yard of The Rose & Crown Hotel, High Street, horses selected for the Hertfordshire Yeomanry are being examined by a veterinary surgeon and, if accepted, 'enlisted' into the Army by branding on one hoof, after which the previous owners would receive payment. [DE/Yo]

The 42nd (Hertfordshire) Company, Imperial Yeomanry was formed in January 1900 at Watford around a nucleus of volunteers from the Hertfordshire Yeomanry Cavalry. They are seen here in High Street, embarking for South Africa in March. After more than a year's hard campaigning and having lost most of its strength to enteric fever or by transfer to other units in South Africa, the company came home only 25 strong in May 1901. [DE/Yo/2/92]

Watford's own Territorial artillery battery, 2nd Hertfordshire Battery Royal Field Artillery, was formed in 1908 and based at the drill hall in Clarendon Road. The battery was at annual camp in Northumberland when ordered to mobilise on 4 August 1914 but returned at once before moving to its 'war station' in Essex. Guns (pulled by six horses) and ammunition wagons (four horses) are seen lined up in Clarendon Road before moving away on 8 August. [RFA collection, John Sainsbury]

When mobilisation was ordered on 4 August 1914 the 1st Battalion the Hertfordshire Regiment were at annual camp in Ashridge Park. Companies returned to their drill halls at once to prepare to move to their 'war stations' in Essex. On 5 August D (Watford) Company left their drill hall in Clarendon Road and are seen here marching to the station, to entrain for what would turn out for many to be four years on the Western Front. [HALS]

The sergeants' mess of the 2nd Hertfordshire Battery, Royal Field Artillery in October 1914. The battery served in France during the winter of 1915/16 and then moved to Egypt. As part of 54th (East Anglian) Divisional Artillery they fought throughout the campaign in Palestine 1917/18, during which Sergeant (later Battery Sergeant Major) Humphries (seated, far left) was awarded the Distinguished Conduct Medal and Sergeant (also later Battery Sergeant Major) Hancock (seated, far right) was mentioned in despatches. [RFA collection, John Sainsbury]

When troops could not be accommodated in barracks or camps they could, under the provisions of the Army Act, be 'billeted' in inns or with families. Here, soldiers of the Norfolk Regiment, just arrived in the Watford area with 54th (East Anglian) Division to prepare for service in Gallipoli, are being allocated billets in Queens Road at the end of May 1915. The Norfolks stayed in Watford until the end of July. [HALS]

The Volunteer Training Corps, which eventually grew into a force similar to the Home Guard of 1940–44, began recruiting in Watford in December 1914 and was active in the town throughout 1915. Their uniform, which was not provided by the government, was of Lovat green, rather than khaki. Members of Watford VTC are seen here filing into a service at St Mary's Church. [Acc 4926]

6th Hertfordshire Cadets, formed under the Territorial and Reserve Forces Act, 1907, in February 1915 at Watford Grammar School. The cadets are pictured here on parade shortly after formation. The boys, aged between 12 and 18, all carry Martini-action carbines but some have yet to be issued with uniform. The unit was recognised as being affiliated to the 1st Battalion of the Hertfordshire Regiment in February 1915. Its establishment was increased to two companies in 1918. Training was suspended in 1920, following an apparent county-wide post-war trend, and the unit disbanded in 1922. [Acc 4926]

Until the formation of the Army Catering Corps in 1941 units were responsible for their own feeding arrangements, usually with a team of 'regimental cooks' under a cook-sergeant. Training facilities were overstretched by the huge increase in the Army after 1914 and any help was welcome – as here, where Mrs Pilling is starting to teach potential cooks of an unidentified unit in her kitchen at 'Inveresk', Hempstead Road, in February 1916. [HALS]

Private S. R. Judge of A Squadron 1st/1st Hertfordshire Yeomanry, a Watford man and pre-war territorial soldier, was awarded the Military Medal for his part in a patrol action during the third – and successful – Battle of Gaza, 7–8 November 1917. The medal is likely to have been presented to him at a ceremony in Watford while he was home on leave and this photograph is believed to have been taken on that occasion. [DE/Yo/2/145]

Local authorities had been encouraged to introduce 'Air Raid Precautions' since 1935. Encouragement was not enough and the Air Raid Precautions Act, which came into force on 1 January 1938, required counties and districts to take all necessary steps, including the recruitment of volunteers for warden, rescue and first aid duties. Here a passer-by takes note of the borough's appeal for volunteers in October 1938. Nearly 2,000 men and women were needed in Watford. [WatLns 0480-00_05]

In 1938 the Watford field artillery battery was expanded and converted into two anti-aircraft batteries. Anti-aircraft units were mobilised several days ahead of others as war loomed in August 1939 to provide cover against expected attack by Germany. During the evening of 24 January, 247 (2nd Watford) Anti-Aircraft Battery, seen here, left their drill hall in Clarendon Road to deploy in defence of RAF Fighter Command Headquarters at Bentley Priory, near Stanmore, Middlesex. [WatGrv 0354-01_27]

The Royal Observer Corps was founded in 1925 as a volunteer organisation for observing and reporting enemy aircraft. The headquarters of the corps' No. 17 Group was established in Watford and from there controlled 34 posts in the surrounding area. From mid-1940 some posts were armed with rifles for local defence and here a sergeant of the 10th Hertfordshire Battalion Home Guard instructs observers on the weapon, probably in 1942. [WatGrv 0467-00_35]

Girls evacuated from Essendine School, London W9, with one of their teachers, arrive at Watford by train in the spring of 1940. Some of the Essendine children were billeted in Kings Langley, others in Dorset and Wales, and the evacuee who would grow up to be celebrity hairdresser Vidal Sassoon, in Wiltshire. Some children remained at Essendine Road for the duration of the war, sheltering in the relative safety of a solid Victorian school building strengthened by the addition of blast walls. It is estimated that Hertfordshire's school population almost doubled at this time – all requiring the provision of homes or education. [WatGrv 0182-01_14]

Hertfordshire's worst air raid occurred in the early morning of 30 July 1944, when a V1 'flying bomb' fell in Sandringham Road, Watford, causing 37 deaths and injuring more than 60 people, many seriously. About 50 houses were damaged beyond repair, while 500 had lesser damage. Here Fire Service, Civil Defence and Home Guard personnel are all on the scene after daybreak. The borough's air raid casualties totalled 60 killed and nearly 150 injured. [Acc 5296]

Opposite, top: 'Invasion exercises' were held regularly between 1941 and 1943 to test the local military defences, almost entirely manned by the Home Guard, together with the full range of Civil Defence services. A mock battle usually took place, often in rather unrealistic conditions, as here, where Home Guard defenders face a small 'enemy' party from Watford hospital's coal heap in September 1942. [WatGrv 0293-00_23]

Opposite, bottom: The Home Guard was raised in May 1940 in the face of imminent invasion. Though at first inadequately armed and trained, the force steadily improved and by the time this photograph was taken it played a key role in Britain's defences. Here men of Watford Borough's 10th Hertfordshire Battalion – then nearly 2,000 strong – wait to have their 'eating irons' washed by Girl Guide volunteer catering assistants at a weekend camp at Russells, July 1943. [WatGrv 0215-00_17]

Members of the WVS serving tea outside Watford Town Hall. The Women's Voluntary Service was founded in 1938, initially to help recruit women into the ARP movement. They assisted civilians during and after air raids by providing emergency rest centres, feeding and first aid. Members also played a part in the evacuation and billeting of children. By the time this photograph was taken in 1943 the organisation had over one million volunteers and was involved in almost every aspect of wartime life. [WatGrv 0539-00_42]

Members of the 15th Hertfordshire (Watford) Company Army Cadet Force assemble at Victoria Boys' School before weekend camp, May 1942. By 1943 the company had an establishment of 200 cadets. The value of pre-call-up training to boys had been identified soon after mobilisation in 1939 and the Hertfordshire Cadet Committee came into being in January 1942. There were 20 new cadet units throughout the county by June of that year. In an attempt to open the ACF to all boys aged 14 to 18, uniform was issued free of charge, but recruits had to supply their own boots. [WatGrv 0032-00-03]

Watford's war memorial in its original position in front of the Peace Hospital. The hospital, conceived of as early as 1917 as a permanent memorial to peace, was opened in 1925. The statues, unveiled at a public ceremony on 18 July 1928 by Lord Clarendon, were the gift and work of sculptress Mary Pownall Bromet, a pupil of Rodin. The artist intended them to symbolise the pain of the bereaved, the maimed survivors of war, and joy and relief for the blessing of peace. The dates 1939–1945 were added after the Second World War. The statues and plinth were moved, as part of a road-widening scheme, to their present position by the Town Hall in 1987. [HALS]

6

TRANSPORT

The Sparrows Herne Turnpike Trust was established in 1762 to maintain 22 miles of road from Bushey Heath, through Watford, Berkhamsted and Tring to Aylesbury (the A41). This plaque near Bushey Arches marks the site of the Lower Watford tollgate where tolls were collected until the abolition of the trust in 1873. In 1823 these were 4½*d* for every horse or beast drawing a coach or wagon, 10*d* for a drove of cows or 5*d* for a drove of sheep. Pedestrians were exempt, as were local waggoners when going to and from Watford market. A milestone directing travellers to Tring and Berkhamsted once stood in the Market Place next to the former National Westminster Bank building. [Wat 0128-00_02]

Unladen barges in Iron Bridge Lock, August 1936. The trestle boards running the length of the boat were used when loading and unloading and were raised on top of the central pillars to provide an all-weather cover for the goods. E. B. Faulkner were based at Leighton Buzzard, Bedfordshire, and these boats, known as 'day boats', were purely commercial, having no living quarters other than a small cabin at the stern. The boys have helped to open the lock gates to allow the boats to leave, possibly for a small reward! [Stg 08975-00]

This early twentieth-century view of Cassio Hamlet, Hempstead Road, evokes the era of the Turnpike Trust as hay carts pass The Horns public house on their way to the High Street. The pub was apparently a favourite stopping place for the carters. In 1756, when it was kept by Hannah Lea, it had stabling for two horses. [WatSerA 0002-00_01]

Opposite, bottom: Laden barges photographed in June 1937. Compare with the picture of the unladen barges. Both boats are nearly ready to be on their way out of the lock once the gates are fully open. The trestle boards are now placed on the central pillars to support the tarpaulin covers. In both pictures the left-hand boat is operated by a woman. [Stg 09482-01]

Colne Bridge was built between 1834 and 1837 to carry the London & Birmingham Railway from Euston over the River Colne at Water Fields. It was originally constructed, at a cost of approximately £10,000, on wooden platforms. The structure was essentially a 'floating' bridge as the top soil structure was sand and gravel. This meant that the track had to be relevelled approximately every two weeks after completion, owing to train weight and subsidence. This picture, taken in 1900, clearly shows the Coal Tax post under the right-hand arch. Duty on coal was much less if carried into London by canal barge than by train. The post marked the taxation boundary. [CV/Wat139]

Opposite, top: Eastbury Road Viaduct formed the 'Bushey Curve' of the London & North Western Railway (later London Midland & Scottish Railway) branch line from Rickmansworth to Bushey and Oxhey. This picture, taken in 1911, clearly shows the wooden 'forms' used in the construction of the brick arches. The Wheatsheaf pub can just be seen bottom right. [HALS]

Opposite, bottom: Watford Junction railway station, pictured here in December 1893, when decorated as part of wedding celebrations for the 7th Earl of Essex and his American wife Adela Grant. Watford Junction station opened on 5 May 1858 initially to serve the London & North Western Railway main line and St Albans branch. It was rebuilt in 1909 and from 1917 until 1982 it was the terminus of London Underground's Bakerloo Line. The present Watford Junction station was the result of a full-scale redevelopment during the 1980s. [HALS]

The first private bus service in Watford, 1898. This was run by the Standard Range and Foundry Company based in Derby Road. [WatLns 0428-00_05]

Opposite, top: Staff of the London & North Western Railway pictured at Watford station in 1905 prior to rebuilding in 1909. With a uniform, competitive wages, structured career progression and the possibility of domestic accommodation, railway service was an attractive occupation to many. Railway service frequently ran in families with sons following their fathers. It may be possible to detect a family resemblance in this picture. [HALS]

Opposite, bottom: One of the buses owned and operated by the London & North Western Railway to provide 'feeder services' to and from Watford Junction station. This one, photographed in about 1900, ran between the station, Market Place and Croxley – the route board visible underneath the middle window above the railway company coat of arms. Note that the conductor has a cash bag and a ticket clipping machine. Tickets were individually numbered and came on a wooden rack, sorted by price, class and destination and were clipped to show purchase. It was some years before driver and upper deck passengers were enclosed against the weather. [Wat 0529-00_06]

Taxicabs began operating in London on 15 March 1907. The General Cab Company purchased 500 new Renault taxis to comply with the Public Carriage Act of 1906 which demanded, among other things, a 25ft turning circle. These taxis are waiting outside the premises of North & Sons in Whippendell Road for their taximeters to be fitted. [Acc 3547]

Watford station on Cassiobury Park Avenue was opened on 4 November 1925. It was designed by C. W. Clark in an Arts and Crafts villa style as part of the London Underground extension from Moor Park. In the early days electricity was supplied by the Metropolitan Underground Railway and services were provided by the Great Central Railway to Marylebone. The line was originally planned with an extension to Watford High Street which was never constructed. Built in conjunction with the great London Underground push into the suburbs universally known as 'Metroland', the houses opposite the station originally sold for approximately £300 each. [Off Acc 1236]

This fire engine, AJH 846, was first registered on 2 May 1935 to a William Walter Lewinson, Watford Corporation, Municipal Office, 14 High Street, Watford. One of the fire engine's first outings was to take part in Watford's Silver Jubilee Parade on Monday 6 May. Cllr W. J. Clarke, Chairman of the Fire Brigade Committee, can be seen standing next to the driver. [Off Acc 1236]

This highly decorated Scammell lorry won second prize in the vehicles section of the Jubilee Day Parade. The prize was £3. Scammell Lorries moved from Spitalfields in East London and originally sold and repaired Foden steam wagons from premises in Tolpits Lane, Watford. The vehicle featured here is a three wheel 'mechanical horse' designed by Oliver North. It had automatic coupling and the single front wheel could be steered through 360 degrees. This example is one of the earlier vehicles manufactured around 1932 as later models had a fully enclosed cab. The Scammell factory closed in July 1988 and the site redeveloped for housing. [Off Acc 1236]

This young man won first prize in the 'Decorated private motor cars – children under 14' category in the 1935 Silver Jubilee parade. He was Gordon Doddrell, with his miniature of Sir Malcolm Campbell's Bluebird racing car. His prize was 10s. The car itself looks rather heavy for a pedal car as it has small spoked road tyres. [Off Acc 1236]

Three members of Watford's Home Guard proudly showing off their motorcycles, *c.* 1939. They were officially described as 'motorcycle orderlies' and their job was to escort convoys through their district, deliver messages and act as reconnaissance. Most used their own bikes and those shown here have civilian registration plates – the one on the left is a Norton and that on the right a Triumph. The trio are wearing standard issue British Army uniform. The central rider may possibly have gained his medal decoration during the First World War as the age for service under the National Services Act of 1939 was between 18 and 41. [WatGrv 0199-00_15]

A lorry belonging to Charles Brightman & Son, builders of Ebury Road, Watford, photographed outside Beechen Grove Baptist Church in 1939. Local firms were often used after bomb attacks for both rescue parties and demolition of unsafe buildings. The satellite type dish is a small searchlight powered by the engine dynamo – useful for work at night. The headlamps do not appear to be fitted with wartime lamp deflectors as the vehicle would have been exempt. The Bedford lorry appears to be a variant of the long wheelbase 30cwt vehicle. [WatGrv 0318-00_25]

This photograph is captioned: 'Willows City of Cardiff Air Ship flying over Watford, March 5th, 1911'. Built in Wales by Ernest Thompson Willows, the *City of Cardiff* made its first flight on 6 August 1910 from Cardiff to White City in London. On 4 November 1910 it left for France and became the first airship to fly to France and the first to fly overnight. It had to make a forced landing near Douai and the French aviator Louis Breguet helped in its repair. Finally arriving in Paris on 28 December, it flew around the Eiffel Tower on New Year's Eve. Willows also made barrage balloons. [HALS]

7

UPSTAIRS, DOWNSTAIRS

High Elms Manor in Garston, a Grade II listed Georgian House, was purchased 'as a wreck' in 1999 by Sheila O'Neill and in 2011 featured in Channel 4's *Country House Rescue*. Throughout the nineteenth century it was owned by various wealthy families. In 1890 it was bought by Claude Watney (of the brewing family) and his wife Ada who changed the name of the property to Garston Manor. A sale brochure of 1932 describes it as 'commanding lovely views over undulating country' and the house included a 37ft-long ball room, billiard room, library, study, thirteen principal bedrooms with a further ten for staff, 'model domestic offices and extensive stores and cellarage'. It was purchased at this date by Colonel William Hilton Briggs and his wife Doris, who was the daughter of local brewery owner Thomas Benskin. Colonel Briggs was managing director of the family company and later its chairman. They moved out in 1946 and the estate was later purchased by the National Health Service and used as a Medical Rehabilitation Centre until its closure in 1997. [Acc 3166]

The main entrance hall and principal staircase of High Elms Manor, c. 1932. The floor is tiled and the walls panelled in mahogany. [HALS]

Sir Edward Hyde Villiers, 5th Earl of Clarendon (1846–1914), photographed in 1905. He served as Lord Lieutenant of Hertfordshire, President and Chairman of the Herts Territorial Association and was an Honorary Colonel in the Herts Yeomanry. He was aide-de-camp to Queen Victoria and became a great friend of the Prince of Wales, later King Edward VII, who frequently stayed with him at his house, the Grove. [HALS]

The Grove occupies an ancient site facing south and overlooking Cassiobury and the town of Watford. This 'noble Queen Anne Mansion' was built in the early eighteenth century and in 1753 was purchased by the Hon Thomas Villiers, Earl of Jersey and British Ambassador to France, who later became the 1st Earl of Clarendon. It has a walled garden and deer park of 130 acres overlooking the valley of the River Gade. [Acc 3166]

The drawing room, *c.* 1920. The family's art collection contained works by Vandyck and Sir Peter Lely, some of which can be seen in these photographs. A sale brochure of 1920 lists 'a suite of seven handsome reception rooms', extensive domestic offices including a school room, 42 bed and dressing rooms, rooms for visiting maids and the batchelors' wing containing a suite of 'six good bedrooms', a servants' hall, boot room, bakehouse and separate laundry block. [Acc 3166]

The library, *c.* 1920. The Villiers family moved out of the Grove around this time and the house was variously used as a gardening school, health centre, riding school and a girls' boarding school. During the Second World War it was the secret wartime HQ for the London, Midland & Scottish Railway. In 1996 it was purchased for renovation as a country house hotel and in 2006 the World Golf Championships, won by Tiger Woods, took place here. [Acc 3166]

George Devereux De Vere Capell, 7th Earl of Essex (1857–1916) photographed in 1893 at the time of his marriage to Adela Grant of New York. The whole town was decorated with British and American flags, including a replica of the Cassiobury Park gateway erected in the Market Place to welcome them home to Watford. He later served with the Imperial Yeomanry in South Africa in 1900–1901 and was an aide-de-camp to King Edward VII. Also a Deputy Lieutenant and Justice of the Peace for Hertfordshire and patron of the living at St Mary's Church, he took a keen interest in local affairs, often hosting celebrations in Cassiobury Park. [WatLns 0605-00_07]

The Countess of Essex and her two lovely daughters, Iris Mary on the left and Joan Rachel, right, photographed in about 1900. At the time of her marriage to the Earl of Essex in December 1893, Adela Grant was reported as 'one of the most beautiful and accomplished American ladies among the many who in recent years have become British peeresses'. [WatLns 0281-00_03]

The central courtyard, *c.* 1922. Cassiobury was rectangular in plan with this open courtyard in the centre. The range at the top is the West Cloister. The principal rooms of the house are to the left, next to and above the Great Cloister, while the buildings on the right housed the domestic offices leading to the kitchen. Here the shrubs and lawns look unkempt and show that the house was probably empty at this time. The view at the top is to the River Gade and canal and shows some of the formal planting in the park. [WatSerB 0016-00_01]

Opposite, top: Cassiobury Park: the north-west elevation photographed in 1922. This shows the main entrance to the house leading into a stone paved and vaulted area known as the West Cloister. [Acc 3166]

Opposite, bottom: Cassiobury Park: the south-west and south-east fronts, in about 1900 which have lovely views over the park. The lawn at the front is laid out for croquet. The game of croquet came to Cassiobury in style in the 1860s when Arthur Algernon, 6th Earl of Essex, hosted croquet parties. It also became a business, as 'Cassiobury Croquet' sets were manufactured by Thomas Turner, his estate manager and carpenter at the estate saw mill. [WatSerB 0007-00_01]

The north-west elevation, *c.* 1922. The main entrance is behind the cedar tree in the centre. To the left of that is an octagonal building which housed the kitchen and led to the laundry building on the far left. The building to the right with gothic arched windows, despite having a cross on the roof, is not a chapel, but housed the principal bedrooms of the house on the first floor. [WatSerB 0008-00_01]

The Great Cloister, *c.* 1922. Leading off the West Cloister through a small vestibule, this area occupied the whole of the southern side of the courtyard. It was meant for recreation and housed a billiard table. Some windows contained coloured leaded glass depicting the family coat of arms and biblical scenes. [WatSerB 0014-00_01]

The Great Dining Room, 1922. Family portraits hang in this room and the walls are panelled. The principal feature is the carving by the famous wood carver Grinling Gibbons who was working at Cassiobury from 1677. The frieze above the fireplace is topped by an eagle with garlands of elaborately carved flowers at each side. [Acc 3166]

The Green Drawing Room, 1922. This room also had gilded carvings by Gibbons and the walls were hung with silk brocade. Perhaps the silk was green, thus giving the name to the room. [Acc 3166]

The Grand Staircase, 1922. This fine staircase had three flights leading to a wide galleried landing on the first floor. Principally carved from oak it is attributed to Edward Pearce working at Cassiobury between 1677 and 1680. It was saved from the demolished house and in 1932 was purchased by the New York Metropolitan Museum of Art where it can still be seen on display. Servants moved upstairs by staircases in other parts of the house. [WatSerB 0034-00_01]

Opposite, top: The Great Library, 1922, one of four libraries in the house as a whole. The walls are lined with books and family portraits. Carving by Gibbons include baskets of fruit and 'probably represent the finest work ever done by Grinling Gibbons'. [Acc 3166]

Opposite, bottom: The Inner Library, 1922. This smaller room led off the Great Library and also held family portraits and fine work by Grinling Gibbons. [Acc 3166]

The Orangery and part of the gardens, *c.* 1900. An orangery is known to have existed at Cassiobury as early as 1669, but a new one was built in about 1801 possibly as part of the landscaping scheme of Humphry Repton. In addition the pleasure grounds had wooded arcades, a rose pergola, two fountains with a lily pond, an Italian pond with dolphin and fig and carnation houses. A walled kitchen garden covered some nine acres, well stocked with fruit trees and there were glasshouses for growing tomatoes, cucumbers, vines and peaches. [WatSerB 0032-00_01]

The main entrance gates to Cassiobury Park on the Rickmansworth Road photographed in June 1937. They were built in about 1802 as the entrance to the main carriage drive to Cassiobury House and housed two families of estate workers. After the creation of the municipal park in 1909 they became a much-loved local landmark, but were demolished in 1970 as part of a road-widening scheme. [Stg 09478-00]

Opposite, bottom: Piles of brick and timber and the very last portion of the house defying demolition, *c.* 1927. Sadly a buyer could not be found for Cassiobury House and the furniture and other contents were sold at auction in 1922. A large portion of the park had already been sold in 1908 for building and in 1909 Watford Urban District Council purchased 65 acres for a public park, which they added to in succeeding years. [WatSerC 0173-00_01]

The Cassiobury Swiss Cottage, *c.* 1922. It stood on the banks of the River Gade and was intended for a family of estate workers. However it was described in 1837 as also providing 'the accommodation of parties during the summer, to take refreshment'. It burned down in the early 1940s. [WatSerA 0009-00_01]

The Cassiobury stables in 1922. They stood to the north-west of the mansion and could house fourteen horses in two blocks. There were also two harness rooms, a loose box, a double coach house and a garage for three cars. Staff could be accommodated above the horses in three bedrooms, with a kitchen and scullery. They were finally demolished in 1937 and sadly horse riding in the park ceased at that date. [Acc 3166 and WatLns 0038-00-01]

8

PUBS & BREWERIES

M. A. SEDGWICK & Co., The Brewery, Watford.

Branch Offices.

LONDON :
3, South Wharf,
Paddington.

UXBRIDGE :
The Colne Brewery.

ALES & STOUT
IN
CASKS
AND
BOTTLES.

Telephone Nos. :
62 WATFORD.
2211 PADDINGTON.
11 UXBRIDGE.

Kindly ask for Price List.

Sedgwick & Co. was a successful old family firm of brewers, neighbours to Benskin in the High Street. Continuously expanding, they owned 65 pubs and off-licences in 1903 and ten years later employed 150 people, with 62 horses and a barge. By the time they sold out to Benskin in 1923, Sedgwick owned 97 pubs. This acquisition increased the Benskin's estate to 700 public houses, by far the largest in Hertfordshire. [DP/117/29/1]

Healey's brewery was founded in 1851 and located in King Street. It was taken over by rivals Benskin in 1898 together with fifteen tied public houses. This late nineteenth-century photograph shows some of the staff posing for the camera. [WatSerC 0184-00_02]

The front of the Benskin's brewery offices decorated for the Silver Jubilee in 1935. The brewery belonging to John Dyson was purchased in 1867 by retired hotel keeper Joseph Benskin. At this date the property included this fine house on the Lower High Street, with a brewery which produced 9,000 barrels each year, and owned 42 public houses and two malt houses. By 1935 Benskin's owned over 800 public houses. In 1957 the company was taken over by Ind Coope but brewing continued in Watford until its closure in 1972. All except the brewery house, which is now the home of Watford Museum, was demolished in 1976. [Off Acc 1236]

The staff of Benskin's brewery who had completed over 30 years' service to the company, photographed in 1933. The oldest, H. J. Brown had been employed for 46 years. Two of the directors, J. Kilby and J. G. Grossman, are seated in the middle of the front row. [Acc 3883]

Benskin's brewery acquired their first Commer truck in 1913. By 1931 there were 59 vehicles in the fleet. This 1934 photograph shows some of the fleet parked around the back of the High Street brewery building that is now Watford Museum. Commer produced a range of commercial trucks, military vehicles and buses from a factory near Luton from about 1907 until 1979. [DP/117/29/1]

Fantastic legends surround the old Eight Bells which stood near St Mary's churchyard until 1956. It was said that body snatchers hid their purloined corpses in the pub's cellar before transporting them to London and that highwaymen drank there. The distinctive sign is now hanging outside The Eight Bells at Saffron Walden, Essex. [Hrt Cpl 0160-00_02]

The Green Man, in the corner of the Market Place next to the former National Westminster Bank building, *c.* 1890. This was kept by Edmund Neal in 1756 but had probably been in existence for more than 100 years at that date. It was rebuilt in the early 1920s but then rebuilt again in 1975 as a shop. [WatLns 0533-00_06]

The Essex Arms Hotel at 69 High Street was used as a magistrates' court in the early nineteenth century. John Thurtell and Joseph Hunt appeared there for the murder of William Weare in 1823. On being sold in 1854 it came with eleven horses, an omnibus, a cow, pig and poultry, a mahogany four-poster bed and two pianos. In this photograph it is part of Trust Houses Ltd. Trust Houses began in 1904 to save declining coaching inns by encouraging them to sell more food and lodging. It closed in 1930 and was demolished to make way for a Timothy Whites dispensing chemist. [WatSerA 0043-00_01]

Few could have mourned the demolition of the High Street pub The Angel in 1910. Incidents of assaults, drunkenness and broken windows were common in the 1890s. In 1897 the pub was described at the Watford Petty Sessions as 'not a high class public house, but lodgings were let there, and it was a very useful institution.' Landlord George Timson was repeatedly fined for selling beer out of hours in the 1860s. This image shows the pub on 8 March 1893. [Acc 3556]

The Crystal Palace beerhouse lasted less than 40 years at 121 High Street before being pulled down in 1907. It was run by George Oram as a sideline to his regular trade as a fruiterer. Oram's shop was sandwiched between that of Lydia Hill, corset maker, and W. E. Pearkes & Sons, house furnishers. Andrew Whitford Anderson took this photograph on 26 June 1907. Watford went through numerous changes in the early twentieth century and Whitford Anderson recorded many of the long-lost buildings in his invaluable collection. [Acc 3556]

The Anglers beerhouse existed for less than a century at 286 Lower High Street. It opened in about 1878 and was kept in 1890 by William Allen. Beerhouses were established in 1830 to try to reduce gin consumption by promoting beer drinking. This photograph dates from 1964 shortly before its demolition. The site is now part of the B&Q depot. [CV/WAT160]

The Leathersellers Arms formerly stood at 235 High Street. To the right of the pub is an antique shop that was run by the parents of Jimmy Perry, the creator of the television series *Dad's Army*. The pub was demolished in 1964 to widen the High Street. Pubs were often used for coroner's inquests. In 1865 an inquest was held at the Leathersellers on Emmanuel Seear, a 45-year-old sawyer who tripped on a nail that had stuck in his shoe and fractured his skull on the wheel of a passing cart. [CV/WAT169]

Dating from the mid-eighteenth century, The One Crown is Watford's oldest surviving public house. The building itself is even older, being a sixteenth-century timber-framed structure, refaced in stucco in the nineteenth century. In 1863 Frederick Hart was arrested for picking the pockets of William Hawkins, who was in a drunken slumber in the tap room. Hart was found not guilty after claiming that if he had stolen the money he would also have taken the empty purse that was still in Hawkins' pocket. [Acc 3883]

The final ever pint was pulled at The White Hart on 3 December 1973, 111 years after it opened. This photograph was taken in 1974, shortly before the pub was lost to a road-widening scheme. It was purchased by brewers, Salter & Co. of Rickmansworth in 1869. The White Hart made the headlines in June 1897 when William Collier was fined for assaulting the landlord Josiah Colley. [Acc 3883]

The Horns in Hempstead Road now bears no resemblance to the original eighteenth-century pub, once a stopping place for carters going to Watford market. It was turned into a live music venue in about 2002. In 1993 an original new sign was erected, depicting an angel blowing a horn on one side, and a horned devil on the other. [Acc 3883]

The Wheatsheaf on Lower High Street boasted a wooden theatre in its back yard, where in 1856 Henry Irving, then an unknown actor, appeared as a member of Holloway's Portable Theatre. It was later known as Barnes's Excelsior Theatre after the pub's landlord George Barnes who died in 1894. The *Watford Observer* described it as 'a link with the earlier Watford in the more leisurely age of the toll gate and the pack horse, before the coming of the trains and motor cars.' It was demolished in 1930 for road widening, shortly after this photograph was taken. Another Wheatsheaf was soon built, but it too was demolished in 1988. [Acc 3883]

Now known as Druids, the Golden Lion in Estcourt Road once had a gold-coloured alabaster lion head as a pub mascot. When the pub was being refurbished in 1952 it was stolen. The thief eventually returned the head in 1996 after he found it while clearing out his garage. It was rehung in exactly the same place as it had been all those years before. [Acc 3883]

Another lost pub of Watford, The Hertfordshire Arms stood at 331 St Albans Road. In 1989 the pub became a training centre for couples wishing to become publicans. They attended a ten-week course, taking exams at the end. It is now a branch of McDonald's. [Acc 3883]

9

EVENTS & CELEBRATIONS

The Diamond Jubilee bonfire, 1897. This giant bonfire was built on Harwoods Farm and a
grand firework display was also held. The men standing from left to right are:
Mr Marcus Boff, Mr Waterhouse, Mr C. P. Ayres, Mr George Capell, Mr F. Fisher and Mr James Darvill.
A procession in the High Street was led by 'the latest invention, a motor cycle bedecked with flowers and
greenery'. [WatDwn 0004-00_01]

The High Street was decorated to celebrate Queen Victoria's Golden Jubilee in June 1887. The town was treated to a procession with several bands, including the Union Workhouse children's band. [WatDwn 0001-00_01]

Opposite, bottom: This must have been a familiar sight in Watford on market day. But on 18 January 1915 the local newspaper reported that a bullock bolted and smashed through the side window of the tailor and outfitter's shop of Arthur Chevis at no. 104 High Street. It emerged via the front window, causing more damage. Luckily neither the bullock nor any people were injured during the incident. [WatSerC 0073-00_01]

On Thursday 27 June 1902 disappointment at the postponement of the coronation of Edward VII and the planned local festivities led to a riot on the streets of Watford. Thirty-five people were arrested, including eight women, and charged with either wilful damage, larceny or assault. A few prisoners were fined, but most received prison sentences of between 14 days and 10 months. Here, a week later, the departing prisoners on their way to St Albans, are being watched by a large crowd. The bonfire that was to be part of the celebrations was set alight, the watchman set upon and his hut wheeled into the flames. Shops, including Mr Longley's drapers, were also attacked and two mounted policemen were pulled from their horses. [WatLns 0516-00_06]

French and Japanese government representatives visiting the Watford Munitions factory in 1917 photographed proudly with their national flags on display. The French delegation included General Ozil and senior French army medical officers aiming to find out more about the effects of chemical weapons. [Acc 4573]

On 17 July 1919 about 350 officers and men of No. 2 Company (St Albans) and the Watford portion of No. 3 Company of the 1st Hertfordshire Regiment were given a banquet in the Clarendon Hall, as part of the Peace celebrations. During the dinner, which was provided by Messrs Buck, Mr Farrington Graves' band played a selection of music. Colonel Sir Charles Elton Longmore proposed a toast to thank the regiment. [Acc 3556]

The peal of eight bells at St Mary's Church waiting to be hoisted up into the tower in 1919. They had been recast by Gillett & Johnson of Croydon. The old seventh bell was originally cast by John Briant of Hertford in 1786, who had also repaired the bell frame at a cost of £93 13s 0d. [WatLns 0125-00_02]

Floods were a frequent occurrence in Watford, particularly in the Lower High Street. The River Colne regularly burst its banks but several attempts to deepen the river by dredging failed. A particularly heavy thunderstorm on Friday 27 July 1906 caused the death of three sheep in Cassiobury Park and the fire brigade had to pump out 3ft of water from the electricity sub-station in Market Street. This photograph was taken in about 1937 and problems continued. Floods in spring 1947 caused such hardship that the mayor set up a relief fund. [WatLns 0426-00_05]

The Watford Silver Jubilee celebrations in 1935 included a carnival and parade with over 150 entries of decorated vehicles, individuals in fancy dress and marching bands. The procession approached a mile in length. The Pedestrians' Fancy Dress Gentlemen's Section was won by F. H. Gurney with his 'Safety First' entry as a Belisha Beacon. He can be seen here towering above the rest as the parade progressed down the High Street. [Off Acc 1236]

These young people representing the British Empire were fourth-place winners of the 'Class 2 Tableaux on Vehicles Non-Trade'. The local newspaper reported: 'Pretty little Miss Margaret Richardson as Rule Britannia, dressed in white and scarlet with a gold helmet on her head and a golden trident in her hand, others in the tableaux represented attendant maids from England, Scotland, Ireland and Wales along with Australia and New Zealand, as well as Girl Guides. John Bull was represented by Irene Beale of North Watford with attendant bulldog loaned by Mr Bedford.' [Off Acc 1236]

On Sunday 12 May 1935 the Watford Jubilee Choir and Orchestra, formed from over 250 local choir members and musicians, performed at the Plaza Cinema. The programme included works by the popular English composers Elgar, Holst and Delius, all of whom had died in 1934. The conductor was Sir Henry Wood, famous for his connection to the London Promenade Concerts ('The Proms'). He died at Hitchin in 1944 and is buried there. [Off Acc 1236]

On Wednesday 18 May 1938 the foundation stone for the New Town Hall was laid. The mayor, Cllr T. Rigby Taylor, was handed a silver trowel by architect Mr C. Cowles-Voysey, with which he laid the cement on to which the stone was lowered. He was then presented with an inscribed mallet by Mr R. E. Costain of Messrs Richard Costain Ltd, to tap the four corners and declare the stone well and truly laid. [Acc 3556]

The Town Hall, constructed on the corner of Rickmansworth Road and the High Street, was built to replace the council offices in Upton Road. Here it is looking very new in 1939 beside a very quiet roundabout. [WatGrv 0047-00_04]

During the month of September 1938 the threat of war loomed. Everywhere towns and villages prepared for war with the provision of air raid shelters and alarms, ready to be used on 1 October if necessary. However, the crisis was averted for the time being to a great sense of gratefulness and relief. A thanksgiving service was held in St Mary's. In the congregation were the mayor and members of the Corporation of Watford. Hymns sung included 'O God, our Help in Ages Past'. [DP/117/29/1]

German visitors from Mainz at Odhams in 1956. Mainz and Watford were twinned in 1956, when both shared a strong connection with the printing and brewing industries. The idea of town twinning gained momentum after the Second World War as a way to rebuild friendships between nations. Mainz is south-west of Frankfurt on the River Rhine, in the wine-growing region of Rhinehessen, Germany. Watford is also twinned with Nanterre, Novgorod, Wilmington and Pesaro. [HALS]

ACKNOWLEDGEMENTS

Many books containing old photographs of Watford have been published, the first by the Borough of Watford's Festival of Britain Committee as early as 1951. Most are now out of print including the two volumes compiled by my former colleague, the Watford Local Studies Librarian Judith Knight, published in 1995 and 1999. Judith used the extensive photographic collection held at Watford Central Library to compile two volumes which delightfully chart the history of the town from about 1880 to 1970. However, there is still a seemingly 'endless interest in old photographs' and the Watford Library collection is vast. Add to these the collections held at Hertfordshire Archives and Local Studies (HALS) at County Hall in Hertford and other private archives in Hertfordshire, and there still exists an extensive supply of images which have never been published in this format before. The compilers of this book have trawled these collections for images not seen before, but we have also included some of our favourite pictures which we could not leave out, either because they are beautiful photographs, or they play an important part in the story of Watford.

This project was begun over a year ago by Dr Jill Barber, former Head of Heritage Services at Hertfordshire County Council. I could not have completed this work without the help of the staff at HALS, many of whom have written captions, scanned images, taken photographs and undertaken very careful research. I particularly wish to thank Nick Connell, Carol Futers, Susan Hall, Gavin Henderson, Paula Mumford, Suzanne Nicholls, Tim Shepherd and Serena Williams. In addition Colonel John Sainsbury added much detail to the 'At War' chapter and Judith Faraday and Linda Moroney, the staff of the Hertfordshire-based John Lewis Archive, have kindly allowed us to use the photographs of Trewins in the first chapter.

Finally in my 'editing hat' I have shamelessly used Judith's work as a mine of information alongside the beautifully produced volumes published by Bob Nunn, without which this book would have been the poorer.

Susan Flood, County Archivist